# A
# Handbook
# for Today's
# Disciples

*For "Suzi"*
*Beloved soul mate of 53 years*
*Companion in Faith*
*Partner in Life*
*urlvd*

FIFTH EDITION

# A Handbook for Today's Disciples

in the Christian Church
(Disciples of Christ)

## D. Duane Cummins

CBP®

ST. LOUIS, MISSOURI

**CBPBooks.com**

Print : 9780827215054

EPUB: 9780827215061     EPDF: 9780827215078

Printed in the United States of America

# Contents

# Acknowledgments

This little volume holds indebtedness far beyond what its modest size may suggest.This 2017 issuing of *A Handbook for Today's Disciples* marks its fifth edition. The first was printed in 1980; the second in 1990; the third in 2000; the fourth in 2010; and, now, the fifth in 2017. The first four editions received a combined 22 printings, with a total circulation to date of 155,000 copies. My first and largest debt is to the membership of the Christian Church (Disciples of Christ) who have acquired and read this little volume across the past four decades. My gratitude to you is enormous.

To W.A. Welsh and Sherman R. Hanson, who originally conceived the idea for this volume and helped shape its character; subsequently to James Suggs and David Polk; then to Cyrus N. White; and now to Brad Lyons and the staff of Chalice Press for their gracious professional assistance in the publication of succeeding editions—I am deeply indebted.

To Walter Giffin, Frank Helme, Lawrence S. Steinmetz, and Howard E. Bowers, I express abiding appreciation for their caring and thorough statistical research in the Office of Research, now the Office of the *Year Book and Directory*. And to Lawrence Steinmetz in particular, who charted the General Assembly resolutions on moral-ethical issues for each edition of the *Handbook*.

To the many manuscript reviewers who examined the various editions for historical accuracy prior to publication—Ronald E. Osborn, Lester G. McAllister, William Fox, Howard E. Short, T. J. Liggett, Kenneth L. Teegarden, A. Dale Fiers, Clark Williamson, Paul A. Crow Jr., Robert A. Thomas, Sharon

Watkins, and D. Newell Williams—my debt is great for their valuable criticisms and insights.

To the authors whose scores of thoughtful works were consulted during the research for this volume—Marcus Borg, Paul Tillich, Harvey Cox, Rudolf Bultmann, Reinhold Niebuhr, Karl Barth, Winfred Ernest Garrison, and an enormous host of others—I express profound gratitude for their insights, and their intellectual and spiritual guidance that shaped the content of this little book.

D. Duane Cummins
Johns Hopkins University
March 1, 2017

CBP gratefully thanks leaders of the Disciples' ethnic ministries for reviewing updates to this Fifth Edition:

- Timothy James, Associate General Minister and Administrative Secretary to the National Convocation
- Chung Seong Kim, Executive Pastor, North American Pacific/Asian Disciples
- Lori Tapia, Interim National Pastor for Hispanic Ministries

# Introduction

A *Handbook for Today's Disciples* has been prepared to help present-day church members understand the heritage, mission, thought, worship, and structure of the Christian Church (Disciples of Christ). It is designed for many uses: as (1) an overview for new members, (2) an updated briefing for veteran members, (3) a synopsis for the casual reader, and (4) a summary guide for study courses on the Christian Church (Disciples of Christ).

The chapters of this volume stand separately. The reader may arrange them in any order and consider them in any sequence desired. Readers unfamiliar with Disciples history would likely be best served by beginning with Chapter One, "The Disciples: A Historical Sketch," because it presents the context within which all subsequent chapters are more easily understood. Those who know the heritage may begin reading wherever they choose.

In the pages that follow, you will discover a storyline of two centuries devoted to the principles of liberty and toleration, a fierce devotion to the integrity of individual choice, and a profound commitment to Christian unity—ultimately evolving into the underlying character of "A Church in Covenant." It is a grand legacy. It is the Disciples legacy, one to be engaged and cherished.

# 1

# The Disciples:
# A Historical Sketch

This is a story with many names—"An American Religious Movement," "The Second Reformation," "A Restoration Movement," "An Experiment in Liberty," "In Search of the Ancient Order," "In Search of Christian Unity," "A Struggle for Reformation"—each adding a measure of definition to the richly varied personality of the subject. It is the story of the Christian Church (Disciples of Christ).

Lines of thought and spirit that give shape to the story extend from distant places in distant times, *and* from nearby in the recent past. They extend from first-century Antioch and Corinth; from eighteenth-century Glasgow and the Scottish Enlightenment; from nineteenth-century Bethany and Cane Ridge; and from the new American nation—often called the "workshop of liberty"—recognized for its egalitarian voice, its pragmatic thought, its enormous belief in the worth and capacity of the individual, and its unwavering adherence to the national ideology of rule by the consent of the governed. These many lines of genesis fashioned the basic instincts and intuitions of the Christian Church (Disciples of Christ).

## 1800–1830: Conception

By 1800, the tumult of the American Revolution was receding in time. Yet the philosophical fires of that Revolution still burned over the meaning of freedom, authority, organization, and leadership. The imprint upon the structures of

1

purpose, and plan of the association, plus an 18-page address or sermon. The Address contained two themes: the quest for Christian unity and the restoration of the principles of the New Testament church. This two-fold plea for restoring the ancient order and pursuing Christian unity was a profound paradox— one the church would never be able to reconcile, one that would ultimately fracture the movement. Still, the *Declaration and Address* laid the foundation for the uniquely American Disciples' religious movement. Its claim to greatness rests not only in its influence on the history of the Disciples but on its place in the history of the ecumenical church. The most widely recited of its thirteen principles was, "That the church of Christ upon earth is essentially, intentionally and constitutionally one."

Within weeks of the document's publication, Thomas Campbell's twenty-one-year-old son, Alexander, arrived in America. Fresh from his university studies at Glasgow, Alexander found himself in full accord with the *Declaration's* call for reform, and quickly discarded much of his Presbyterian experience. He soon displaced his father as leader of the tiny community of reformers. The Christian Association reconstituted itself as the Brush Run Church in 1811, adopting a scriptural format of several New Testament precepts:

- Christ, the bedrock of faith and head of the church.
- The Bible, sole authority, with emphasis on the New Testament.
- Baptism by immersion and for responsible believers.
- The Lord's Supper, celebrated weekly.
- Government, vested in congregational leadership, with little distinction between clergy and laity.
- Union of all Christians; one body, one faith, one God—that all may be one.

The Brush Run congregation was loosely federated with the Redstone Association of Baptists. On August 30, 1816, Alexander Campbell delivered his now celebrated *Sermon on the Law* at Cross Creek, boldly proclaiming that Christians lived under grace, not law; under Christ, not Moses; under the New Testament, not the Old. This breach of Baptist doctrine soon resulted in the dismissal of the Brush Run reformers from the Redstone Association. Untroubled, the little congregation continued its life in associational relationship with the neighboring Mahoning Baptist Association, which it had joined before its Redstone termination.

During the crowded years of the 1820s, the Stone and Campbell movements broke out of the geographic provincialism that had stunted their respective reforms. Following a decade of largely unnoticed labor, Alexander Campbell engaged in a series of widely publicized debates, published a Christian hymnal along with a modern version of the New Testament, and inaugurated the circulation of a periodical: *The Christian Baptist* (est. 1823). Stone published a periodical of his own, *The Christian Messenger* (est. 1826), and opened an acquaintance with Campbell. Late in the decade, Walter Scott, a newly arrived Scottish Highlander, began work as an evangelist for the Mahoning Association, to promote the Reform Movement. Through a magnetic and populist appeal, Scott (Voice of the Golden Oracle) won thousands of former Baptists to the reform and earned status as one of the founding figures of the Disciples' Movement. Scott's extraordinary evangelism unlocked parochial shackles and gave the Movement its freedom to expand and grow.

Ousting Campbell-Scott reformers from Baptist associations became common sport. By action at Austintown, Ohio, in 1830, the Mahoning Baptist Association voted to dissolve itself. Although the Brush Run reformers and the Baptists could not achieve harmonious consensus on the issues of faith and polity, the dissolution was still unexpected. The event is recognized as a milestone in the history of the Reform Movement. From that moment, the reformers were clearly independent, no longer functioning in association with an established denomination, and henceforward distinctively identified as Disciples, rather than Baptists.

## 1830–1866: The Infant Years

*The Millennial Harbinger,* authored and edited by Alexander Campbell, first appeared in 1830, replacing the former *Christian Baptist.* The *Harbinger,* more temperate toward the need for church structure, carried hints of an awakening sense of social responsibility in Campbell's thinking, helping to ease the way for eventual union with the movement initiated by Barton Stone. Despite a few testy editorial exchanges with Stone, Campbell ultimately supported the idea of union between their kindred groups, an idea formally launched on January 1, 1832, at Hill Street Christian Church in Lexington, Kentucky.

*Disciples* and *Christians* began the delicate process of becoming one. They found common ground in rejecting human creeds, accepting the centrality of Christ in their faith, recognizing the supreme authority of scripture, and proclaiming their mutual desire for union. The matters of evangelism, concepts of ministry, frequency of communion, and form of baptism initially resisted resolution but were eventually reconciled. The more substantive issues of balancing liberty and order, and faith and reason, remained in creative tension. Irresolution also remained on the lesser question of an appropriate name. Campbell insisted upon the use of *Disciples* as a more historic, scriptural, and descriptive identification. Stone was equally insistent upon the use of *Christians,* the term tending to prevail in the names of congregations.

Growth characterized the decades of this period. Union, achieved congregation by congregation during the early Thirties, joined some ten thousand Christians and twelve thousand Disciples. Reaching out from its regional base, the Stone-Campbell reform soon spanned the continent. During the 1830s, new congregations took root in Detroit, Baltimore, Dubuque, and Little Rock; in Brownville, Nebraska, and Bowie County, Texas; in Indiana, Illinois, and Missouri. The California and Oregon trails carried scores of "Campbellites" to the far West during the overland migrations of the Forties and Fifties. And, in 1843, *The Millennial Harbinger* announced the attendance of delegates representing the 16 congregations in Ontario, Canada, at Norval—the first evidence of cooperation. Formal cooperation between Canadian Disciples and the ACMS (American Christian Missionary Society) subsequently began in 1853. By 1860, the Movement exhibited national and international proportion, with a membership of nearly 200,000 in 2,100 congregations. Yet it achieved relatively little headway east of the Alleghenies, especially in New York and New England.

Order was the theme of the 1840s. Prompted by the demand for informed and responsible leadership within the congregations of the rapidly expanding movement, Alexander Campbell published a second edition of his compendium of Disciples beliefs, *The Christian System,* and donated land upon which he founded Bethany College for the purpose of educating a cadre of lay leadership. Attempting to develop a structured means of cooperation among the many congregations, Campbell initiated a decade-long series of articles in the *Harbinger* on the controversial subject of church organization.

By 1840, members of some congregations had begun to gather for fellowship in state "conventions," and, in 1849, the first national gathering of the Movement convened in Cincinnati, with 156 delegates from one hundred churches in eleven states. The convention approved the formation of the American Christian Missionary Society in the hope of achieving a greater sense of national cooperation and international vision. While the creation of a structure beyond the congregation stirred opposition among those who thought such a structure violated a basic principle of the movement, others welcomed it as a much-delayed recognition of corporate responsibility for a larger mission.

Confronted with the peculiar institution of slavery, reformers sought a nondivisive position. They were led to the notion that the issue was a matter of opinion, not faith, and therefore not a test of fellowship. Campbell believed his unyielding commitment to "unity" was a higher obligation than his unequivocal opposition to slavery. While most mainline denominations were structurally fractured by the economic, social, and political devastation of the Civil War, Disciples forestalled that fate because of their inherent organizational elasticity and their commitment to the freedom of individual choice. Fissure, however, remained–barely below the surface– and, with the death of Alexander Campbell on March 4, 1866, a new generation was left to struggle with internal tensions.

## 1866–1917: Adolescent Years

The founders were in their graves. Barton Stone died in 1844, Thomas Campbell in 1854, Walter Scott in 1861, and Alexander Campbell in 1866. Still under the rule of its two-fold plea to restore the ancient order and to build Christian unity, the Movement entered upon a new forty-year journey, marked by dramatic numerical growth, budding denominational consciousness, and a deepening internal division of thought.

A choice of direction inevitably confronts the second generation of all reforms. The Stone-Campbell Movement had to decide if it should cement its conservative views and hold solidly to traditions of the ancient order; or if it should venture into Christian unity, intellectual freshness, change, flexibility, and adaptation of its ministry to the newly emerging socio-cultural-economic environment of post-Civil War America–the profound paradox of the two-fold plea. Choosing between these two directions was compounded by the lingering bitterness of the Civil War. The leaders, lacking the personal force of the founders, were not able to consolidate the membership. Part of the Movement veered one direction, part of it went the other way, and they were never reconciled.

Surface battles within the Movement were fought on several questions: Did the New Testament forbid or permit the use of instrumental music in worship? Did it permit or forbid the organization of missionary societies beyond the congregation? Did it forbid or permit the development of a professional ministry with title and authority? The battles raged for forty years, but, in the end, it was the deeper dissension over the two-fold plea that severed the relationship. The Churches of Christ, concentrated in the former Confederate states, followed the first path in pursuit of the ancient order. The Disciples of Christ, concentrated in the upper Midwest, followed the second path in pursuit of Christian unity. The initial separate listing of the two groups in the 1906 Federal Religious Census was little more than a statistical event, since their choice of separate ways had long since been authenticated.

Between the Civil War and World War I, four important ministries took form within the Disciples' Movement. The **first** was journalism. Always abundant in editors, the Disciples were particularly fortunate to be influenced in this period by the progressive insights of Isaac Errett, editor of the *Christian-Standard,* and J.H. Garrison, editor of *The Christian Evangelist,* a weekly periodical later succeeded by a monthly called *The Disciple,* and then *DisciplesWorld.* The **second** ministry was a pioneering missionary initiative, parented by the leadership of Caroline Neville Pearre and Archibald McLean. The formation of the Christian Woman's Board of Missions and the Foreign Christian Missionary Society in 1874–75, coupled with the development of the National Benevolent Association in 1877, provided a means of outreach and contact with the larger world. The **third** ministry was higher education. Disciples, along with several other denominations, reactivated the long religious tradition of intellectual leadership that the new revivalism had weakened. The founding of more than four hundred Disciples-related educational institutions produced a more informed laity, as well as a better educated clergy, and educators soon exercised considerable influence upon the thought and practice of the Movement. The **fourth** ministry was cooperation with other communions. Disciples participated in the development of uniform lessons through the International Sunday-School Association in 1872, joined the International Council of Religious Education, were charter members of the Federal Council of Churches, and, due to the creative foresight of Peter

Ainslie, originated the Council on Christian Union in 1910. These four ministries enlivened and enlarged Disciples vision.

While these four ministries were invaluable in stretching late nineteenth-century Disciples thought, they were not able to overcome the cultural and intellectual limitations of a rural confinement or successfully bridge the chasm between church and society. Consequently, the Movement, like much of American Protestantism, was not adequately prepared to address the new social heterogeneity, to assimilate the growing tides of immigrants, to adjust to the rapidly developing urban-industrial complex, or to hear the public distress over social ethics, poverty, and a host of related issues. It remained essentially a rural, county-seat-town Movement, stunted in its social witness by an overriding commitment to unity.

When the Disciples celebrated the centennial of the *Declaration and Address* in 1909, they numbered 1,250,000 members, largely the result of their effective evangelism in the context of the second and third religious awakenings. In spite of division and cultural isolation, they enjoyed phenomenal growth, but "restoration of the ancient order" became a more elusive and less hallowed goal in the new socioeconomic order.

### 1917–1968: Drive to Maturity

By the end of the First World War, the marrow and sinew of the Movement were in place. With their physical growth stabilized, Disciples entered a time of intellectual refinement and structural consolidation.

The most telling influence upon Disciples during these years came from a new theology advocating thorough historical research of the scriptures and an intellectual awareness of contemporary cultural trends. After many years of controversy between the "new liberals" and the orthodox defenders of an insulated Biblicism, the exponents of each view became locked in open rivalry for control of the College of the Bible at Lexington, Kentucky. The outcome of the 1917 hearings, which amounted to a heresy trial, established the new theology as the predominant intellectual force among Disciples for the next forty years. Among the effects of this theological shift was a waning of the concept of unchanging applicability of New Testament precedents and a release from the tunnel vision of the one-hundred-year effort to "restore the ancient order." Exemplars of this new theological position–Herbert L. Willett, Edward Scribner Ames, Winfred E. Garrison, and Charles Clayton Morrison–were among the influential architects of Disciples thought during the first half of the twentieth century.

An additional consequence of the controversy was the gradual withdrawal from Disciples by those who thought the Stone-Campbell Movement had forsaken its heritage. This group eventually numbered 650,000 members and moved to final separation during the days of discord surrounding "restructure" in the late 1960s. Separation actually began at the time of the 1926 International Convention in Memphis–when a rump group convened in the Pantages Theater, where the North American Christian Convention first organized–and ultimately concluded with a separate 1971 yearbook listing for the Christian Churches and Churches of Christ.

The unending search for more efficient organization led to the 1917 establishment of the International Convention of the Disciples of Christ. Likewise, the United Christian Missionary Society was created in 1920, unifying six independent boards into a single church agency. These reconstituted organizations served Disciples ministry through the post-war 1920s, the economic depression of the 1930s, and the Second World War in the 1940s. Many other agencies and committees were developed along the way. The most widely known grew out of the fellowship concept and included the Christian Youth Fellowship (1944), the Christian Women's Fellowship (1949), and the Christian Men's Fellowship (1951).

The post–World War II proliferation of organized agencies within the movement produced confusion. Near the end of the 1950s, a Panel of Scholars, composed of seventeen Disciples minds, was commissioned to reexamine Disciples precepts in light of the new religious vitality of that day. The Panel Report, completed and published in 1963, softened the old rigidities of Disciples' thought on theology and church structure. Simultaneously, the International Convention, meeting in 1960 in Louisville, Kentucky, brought into existence the Commission on Brotherhood Restructure, directing it to create a new form of organization rooted in something more substantive than a simple coalition of autonomous agencies, fellowships, congregations, committees, and conventions. The Restructure Commission, under the leadership of Granville T. Walker, A. Dale Fiers, and Kenneth L. Teegarden, labored throughout the religiously disillusioned Sixties, producing a concept of "Church" and a unique "covenantal" design—a *Church in Covenant*. A representative Assembly meeting at Kansas City in 1968 overwhelmingly approved *The Provisional Design for the Christian Church (Disciples of Christ)*.

The proliferation of agencies among twentieth-century Disciples was accompanied by a growing diversity of cultural expressions, each organized into separate structures while maintaining representation within the Disciples' core *Design*. And each produced saintly Disciples leaders, revered by the entire church—including Preston Taylor, Domingo Rodriguez Figueroa, and David Kagiwada.

Structure for African Americans evolved from the first post-Civil War National Convention of "Colored" Disciples in 1867. By 1917, the group had become the National Christian Missionary Convention and in that year, following an ill-fated incorporation attempt with the new International Convention, it became an auxiliary of the convention. In 1943 and again in 1955 plans were proposed for merging the work of the National Christian Missionary Society with the work of the United Christian Missionary Society within the International Convention. The merger was ultimately completed with the UCMS in 1960 and with the International Convention in 1969 through a resolution that proclaimed merger under the disciplines of the "ONE God, in ONE church and stand united in ONE mission in the world." The same resolution then called for the creation of a *National Convocation* "to provide an instrumentality within the structure of the Christian Church (Disciples of Christ)." This instrumentality elects its own twenty-four member board of trustees, employs an administrative secretary (Associate General Minister), and holds biennial assemblies for its more than 400 congregations.

Likewise, *Obra Hispana* (Hispanic ministries), serving approximately 200 congregations, reached the 115th anniversary of the founding of the first Hispanic Disciples congregation in San Antonio, Texas, 1899. The Hispanic and Bilingual Fellowship, known as the *Obra Hispana,* is currently structured around six conventions (regions) that meet biennially in Assembly. The Central Pastoral Office for Hispanic Ministries, established in 1992, serves Hispanic congregations "in collaborative partnership with Disciples general ministries, regional offices, and Hispanic conventions." A National Pastor (elected by the Hispanic National Assembly) manages the Central Pastoral Office with the responsibility of providing pastoral care, education, and development, and raising funds from Hispanic congregations, the Disciples Mission Fund, and other church sources. A twenty-member board of directors, four-fifths of whom are elected by the conventions, gives oversight to the *Obra Hispana,* in addition to the Pastoral Commission, which includes the board and four appointed General Board representatives, two from the Administrative Committee and two Regional Ministers.

The *North American Pacific/Asian Disciples* received its present name in 1996. NAPAD has eighteen different ethnic and linguistic groups. They are Burmese, Cambodian, Chin, Chinese, Chuukese, Filipino, Indian, Indonesian, Japanese, Karen, Korean, Laotian, Mongolian, Montagnard, Samoan, Tongan, Vietnamese, and Zo. The lineage of NAPAD extends back more than 110 years to the first Chinese missions on the West Coast during the 1890s. The first Japanese congregation was organized in Los Angeles in 1908; the first Filipino congregation was founded in 1933, also in Los Angeles; and the first Korean congregation appeared in 1976, again in Los Angeles. Following a series of Indianapolis consultations in 1978–79, the Fellowship of Asian American Disciples was organized, later changing its name to American Asian Disciples. In 1991 an Asian staff person–Executive Pastor for North American Asian Ministries–was employed by the Division of Homeland Ministries to focus exclusively on Asian ministries. In January 2010 NAPAD structurally separated itself from Disciples Home Missions (formerly Division of Homeland Ministries), and–like *Obra Hispana*–became a collaborative partner with the Disciples general ministries, managing its ministry through a fifteen-member board of directors and Executive Pastor. NAPAD convenes its membership in a biennial convocation.

## Since 1968: A Church in Covenant

Approval of the *Provisional Design* marked the passage of Disciples into a denomination. Officially named the Christian Church (Disciples of Christ), they became a church.

The genius of the *Design* was lodged in the concept of covenant. Through covenant, the congregations, regions, and general agencies were linked in an interdependent and mutually supportive relationship, working in concert, none the mere servant of the other, all accountable to each other. Through covenant, the church was able to achieve a more equitable balance between some of its ageless polarities–"freedom and community," "unity and diversity," "congregationalism and catholicity." Through covenant, the church was able to minister more effectively to a post-Protestant society and to pursue more confidently its venerable goal of Christian unity. The "Church in Covenant" produced its first Order of Ministry in 1971; and covenant has helped lift the church beyond ideological and theological narrowness. The mutual affinity and pervasive bond among tens of thousands of Disciples, expressed through covenant, is entered voluntarily and in love.

The new covenantal *Design* worked through a ten-year period of implementation, culminating in 1977 with the removal of the term *provisional* from the *Design* and the decision to proceed without the writing of a formal constitution. A. Dale Fiers was elected the first General Minister and President (1968–1973) of the restructured church; his successors included Kenneth L. Teegarden (1973–1985), John O. Humbert (1985–1991), Richard L. Hamm (1993–2003) and Sharon Watkins (2005–2017). From 1990 to 2017 the Disciples ministered under severe financial constraint due to declining membership coupled with weakness in stewardship and a near dysfunctional system of financial distribution. Disciples absorbed the closure of a university, the bankruptcy of one general ministry, the misappropriation of funds by another general ministry, mismanagement of resources within two regions, along with the discontinuance of its major periodical–*Disciples World.* It was a time of testing the strength and resilience of a "Church in Covenant." Participating membership in the Christian Church (Disciples of Christ) numbered about 274,000 in 2016–a time of growing religious pluralism, an environment marked by a new-age, post-modern search for individual spirituality, an age of disaffection from mainline Protestant institutional religion (Methodist, Presbyterian, American Baptist, United Church of Christ, Episcopal, Lutheran, and Disciples) whose share of the total religious membership in the United States in 2015 had dropped to 13 percent. Disciples–despite the common characterization of Mainline Protestantism as "low on funds, low on energy, and low on morale,"–view themselves as still youthful in historical experience, with much creative power yet to be tapped. They remain driven by their passion for Christian unity, and compelled to transcend and transform the challenges of the early twenty-first century, clearly manifested in the four priorities guiding the ministry of the church: becoming a pro-reconciling/anti-racist church; forming 1000 new congregations by the year 2020; transforming 1000 current congregations by

both embodied in the widely recited New Testament notion of the "parental imagery" of God, a notion that has long dominated popular Christian thought.

Equally dominant, with a powerful hold on the human mind, is the concept of "Supernatural Theism,"–involving a "Theistic God" leading a separate existence; or a Supreme Being "up there" beyond the universe; or an authoritarian figure revealing how humans should live and what they should believe, issuing discipline and reward to humans according to their behavior.

It is from Psalm 139, said to be the most searching meditation in all literature on the meaning of God, that much of traditional theology about God has been developed. In recent times, some theologians have offered refinement to the ways of thinking about God through reinterpreting Psalm 139, suggesting the word *God* expresses the ultimate "depth of all our being," that God is not a separate being, but "being" itself. The image of "depth" redirects human perception away from the surface or edges of life, away from a separate God entity "out there," turning our focus toward the deepest "Ground of Being"–the dwelling place for the gifts of human excellence: truth, hope, grace, love, benevolence, justice, mercy–humanity. It is said that when a person touches the "Ground of Being," that person touches God; his or her humanity becomes endowed with the meaning of God; divinity, it is said, is the ultimate depth of humanity.

Other theologians of our time cite the apostle Paul's famous words from his sermon to the Athenians–that God is that in which *"we live and move and have our being"* (Acts 17:28a)– suggesting God is "an encompassing spirit," the life we live, the love we share; God is the power and source of life within us, the life force revealed in us and through us. These theologians point to the spirit within the core and depth of every life as the presence of God in humanity. Paul is cited once again: *"[We have received] the Spirit that is from God so that we may understand the gifts bestowed on us from God"* (1 Cor. 2:12); *"The fruit of the*

*Spirit is love, joy, peace, patience, kindness, generosity, faithfulness, gentleness"*(Gal. 5:22–23a); and, finally, *"Your body is a temple of the Holy Spirit within you, which you have from God"*(1 Cor. 6:19)!

## Disciples' Traditions

All attempts to define God reflect human limitations. Disciples, while not given to defining God, usually think of God as revealed through the life of Jesus Christ. Many writers cite transcendent human attributes such as the sense of moral obligation, the presence of conscience, the capacity for thought and reason, the capacity to appreciate beauty, the capacity for self-transcendence, the power to love, and the ability to know justice, honesty, mercy, and happiness as rational proofs of the existence of God in persons. Disciples do not reject reasonable evidences of God's existence and they believe that intellect must support the foundations of faith; but neither do they limit their understanding of God to rational definition. They view God as beyond definition, inexpressible, a supreme mystery that transcends time and geography, a force greater than all the energies shooting through nature—more than a magnification of human powers. To reduce God solely to rational proof eliminates the role of *faith*, which is the Disciples' posture toward the mystery. Disciples affirm the reality of God in the world but resist the temptation to enclose God in human definition.

## Disciples' Affirmations

We rejoice in God, maker of Heaven and Earth.

THE DESIGN

## Scriptures

*In the beginning when God created the heavens and the earth…*

GENESIS 1:1

*"I AM WHO I AM."… "[S]ay to the Israelites, 'The LORD, the God of your ancestors, the God of Abraham, the God of Isaac, and the God of Jacob, has sent me to you':*
*This is my name forever, / and this my title for all generations."*

EXODUS 3:14–15

*In Christ God was reconciling the world to himself...*

2 CORINTHIANS 5:19

*Dear friends, let us love one another, because love is from God. Everyone who loves is a child of God and knows God, but the unloving know nothing of God. For God is love.*

1 JOHN 4:7–8 (NEB)

*In the beginning was the Word, and the Word was with God, and the Word was God. He was in the beginning with God. All things came into being through him, and without him not one thing came into being. What has come into being in him was life, and the life was the light of all people...*
*And the Word became flesh and lived among us, and we have seen his glory, the glory as of a father's only son, full of grace and truth.*

JOHN 1:1–4, 14

*You have searched me and known me... / You...are acquainted with all my ways... / Where can I go from your spirit? / Or where can I flee from your presence?... / If I take the wings of the morning / and settle at the farthest limits of the sea, / even there your hand shall lead me... / For it was you who formed my inward parts... / How weighty to me are your thoughts, O God! / How vast is the sum of them!*

PSALM 139:1, 3, 7, 9–10A, 13A, 17

# Jesus Christ

### General Briefing

Verses opening the first chapter of John's gospel announce that Jesus is the "Word of God" become flesh, embodied in a human life. The historical circumstances of his life reveal the human Jesus of Nazareth. The infusion of God into this person added a dimension identified as the *Christ* (a Greek word meaning "the anointed one," or "the Messiah,") that Christians recognize and confess through faith. The joining of God with humanity in the person of Jesus Christ forms the very heart of the Christian faith. Although the question of Jesus Christ being divine or human or both confounds human wisdom, it is this union of "humanity" and "divinity"–the uniting of the historical

Jesus with the Christ of faith into a single being—that expresses the fundamental claim of Christianity.

The Jesus of history is known through many sources. Fragments of New Testament papyri from more than twenty gospels recovered in the sands of Middle Eastern deserts attest to the life of the human Jesus. Chronicles of old, including the *Antiquities* of Josephus (93 C.E.), the *Annals* of Tacitus (110 C.E.), and the *Lives of the Twelve Caesars* by Suetonius (98 C.E.), all contain historical references to Jesus. And, in our own time, the discoveries of archaeology and exegesis have resulted in more being written on the life of Christ in the last fifty years than in the previous nineteen and one-half centuries. Ecclesial and secular scholars agree that Jesus of Nazareth has been the dominant figure in the history of Western culture for twenty centuries, shaping its calendar and its major cultural holidays. He is the center of Christian thought, worshiped by billions, celebrated weekly in church liturgies.

The cold, historical content of Jesus' human life can be sketched in broad strokes. His earthly existence, beginning in the days of Herod and ending in the time of Pilate, has been fixed with relative accuracy. A carpenter by trade, his hometown was the community of Nazareth in Galilee, a province of Palestine where he lived for nearly 35 years. During the final years of his brief life, a religious fervor touched the Jordan Valley, drawing Jesus out of Nazareth and into an extraordinary ministry. He was baptized by John the Baptist, then taught in towns and villages along the shores of the Sea of Galilee. Although his ministry challenged both secular and religious uses of power, many of his contemporaries mistook his ministry as exclusively a political threat, a misapprehension that led to his arrest and execution.

It is the *character,* rather than the biography, of this man that is known with thoroughness. He was called the *Christ.* The apostle Paul used the term again and again in his several letters describing the spiritual power of Christ for a generation who had not known the human Jesus in the flesh. The Gospels, written during the decades after the letters of Paul and written specifically to proclaim the divinity of Christ, are laden with anecdotes that reveal the depth of his divine nature—making his life timeless, revelatory, and transcendent. Filled with the grace of God, Jesus performed unending good works, turning all things base into things noble. His moral teachings have been called the most benevolent in all of history; and his Sermon on the Mount is viewed as a summary of true religion. Theologians say the essence of Jesus' character draws all lives into a new humanity, making known to all the meaning of life.

The very name "Jesus Christ" affirms the uniting of his humanity with the grace of God. For Christians, the crucifixion is the point at which the Christ of Faith and the Jesus of History are joined. The human Jesus died at the crucifixion, but the Christ of faith was resurrected into a new life of the spirit, a new dimension of life not subject to death. The dying and resurrection of Jesus Christ, declare theologians, should be seen by believers as a symbol of their own personal transformation, dying to an old identity and way of being in this world, and rising to or entering into a new identity and way of being centered in Christ's message of justice, mercy, and love—in Paul's words: "becoming a new creation in Christ." In this way the resurrection provides for all generations the experience of faith in the Lord, Jesus Christ.

### Disciples' Traditions

"No Creed but Christ!" This phrase rings across the pages of Disciples' history, heralding the belief that faith in Jesus Christ is a personal faith. Thomas and Alexander Campbell, along with Barton Stone, taught that creeds were divisive and that scripture alone was sufficient for faith in Jesus Christ.

The evolution of thought among Disciples regarding the humanity and divinity of Christ began with heavy emphasis upon the divine authority of the Christ of faith. Nineteenth-century preoccupation with the divinity of Christ overpowered the human Jesus, causing the Jesus of Nazareth to be generally ignored, but throughout the twentieth century and into the twenty-first, Disciples' thinking has experienced a steadily growing turn toward the life and teachings of the historical Jesus.

In our own time, Disciples have achieved a good balance in their thinking on the humanity and divinity of Jesus Christ. Disciples think of Jesus first as human, and then find in this individual the most complete, the most sublime, the most thoroughly moral personality the world has ever known. His was a life "full of grace and truth," the manifestation of what humanity can become. It is supremely the place in which we see God—in the mercy, the love, the compassion, the justice, and the will of Jesus Christ. Here is revealed God! The Christ of faith becomes a reality for all generations through the grace of God in Jesus. It brings us to confess gladly with those many generations before—"Jesus is the Christ, the Son of the living God."

## Disciples' Affirmations

We confess that Jesus is the Christ, the Son of the living God, and proclaim him Lord and Savior of the world.

THE DESIGN

## Scriptures

*He said to them, "But who do you say that I am?" Simon Peter answered, "You are the Messiah, the Son of the living God." And Jesus answered him, "Blessed are you, Simon son of Jonah! For flesh and blood has not revealed this to you, but my Father in heaven."*

MATTHEW 16:15–17

*And the Word became flesh and lived among us, and we have seen his glory, the glory as of a father's only son, full of grace and truth.*

JOHN 1:14

*But these are written so that you may come to believe that Jesus is the Messiah, the Son of God, and that through believing you may have life in his name.*

JOHN 20:31

*"Anyone who has seen me has seen the Father."*

JOHN 14:9 (NEB)

*He is the image of the invisible God, the firstborn of all creation; for in him all things in heaven and on earth were created, things visible and invisible, whether thrones or dominions or rulers or powers—all things have been created through him and for him. He himself is before all things, and in him all things hold together. He is the head of the body, the church; he is the beginning, the firstborn from the dead, so that he might come to have first place in everything. For in him all the fullness of God was pleased to dwell, and through him God was pleased to reconcile to himself all things, whether on earth or in heaven, by making peace through the blood of his cross.*

COLOSSIANS 1:15–20

# The Holy Spirit

### General Briefing

The search for the meaning of the Holy Spirit has continued throughout the entire history of Christianity. The prevailing view, common to many religious bodies, is that the Holy Spirit is one member of a trinity, co-existing with the Father and the Son in a single union—one God manifest in three ways. This view rests primarily on the writings of Paul, who explained that the Holy Spirit provides the means to understand the presence of the risen Christ in each believer and in the church. The Holy Spirit, in Paul's view, is separate from Christ, yet is the spirit of Christ, and it is the vehicle that unites the believer and the church *with* Christ. All Christians, stated Paul, who accept the gospel and are baptized will know the joy of the Spirit dwelling within them.

Paul was often called to elaborate upon his teaching about the Holy Spirit. The community of Christians at Galatia generally ignored any notion of Spirit and drifted toward the legalistic doctrines of the past. Paul urged them to cultivate the sense of spirit; otherwise, their religion would harden and die. By contrast, the community of Christians at Corinth carried the meaning of Spirit to excess, which brought counsel from Paul to guard against developing a spiritually gifted elite and to because the discernment of truth is lodged in the Bible's underlying spirit rather than its literal events. The truth of the Bible is its "more than literal," meaning. Metaphor, parable, and symbolism convey "meaning," rather than a factual report. It is not faith in the book that Christians hold, but faith in the grace of God as revealed through the book.

## Disciples' Traditions

Seated in crude frontier meetinghouses and gathered in forest clearings, the early Disciples dedicated themselves to hearing, reading, and studying the Scriptures. Their religious faith and vision of church were solidly rooted in the New Testament, with particular reference to the *Acts of the Apostles*. Barton Stone believed that God worked through the testimony of Scripture. Alexander Campbell believed that careful historical study of all biblical writings strengthened each believer's faith. He objected to treating the Bible like a "Leviticus manual or a rigid primitivist pattern"; rather, he urged openness to the fresh revelation to be derived from studying the word by what was called the historical-grammatical method, a precursor to what is known today as the historical-critical method.

Disciples do not have an "official" interpretation of the Bible. Individuals are encouraged to interpret the Scriptures in the light of all sciences and through the insight of Christian tradition. Because the Bible is viewed as human testimony of divine revelation, and evolved through long periods of oral transmission—and, later, a score of translations and revised versions—Disciples tend away from a literal, inerrant approach and more toward an understanding that combines both faith and reason. Disciples do not have distinctive doctrines.

## Disciples' Affirmations

Where the scriptures speak, we speak; where the scriptures are silent, we are silent.

SERMON BY THOMAS CAMPBELL, 1809

Within the universal church we receive…the light of scripture.

THE DESIGN

## Scriptures

*From childhood you have known the sacred writings that are able to instruct you for salvation through faith in Christ Jesus. All scripture is inspired by God and is useful for teaching, for reproof, for correction, and for training in righteousness, so that everyone who belongs to God may be proficient, equipped for every good work.*

2 TIMOTHY 3:15–17

*So we have the prophetic message more fully confirmed. You will do well to be attentive to this as to a lamp shining in a dark place, until the day dawns and the morning star rises in your hearts.*

2 PETER 1:19

*We declare to you what was from the beginning, what we have heard, what we have seen with our eyes, what we have looked at and touched with our hands, concerning the word of life—this life was revealed, and we have seen it and testify to it, and declare to you the eternal life that was with the Father and was revealed to us—we declare to you what we have seen and heard so that you also may have fellowship with us; and truly our fellowship is with the Father and with his Son Jesus Christ. We are writing these things so that our joy may be complete.*

1 JOHN 1:1–4

*Since many have undertaken to set down an orderly account of the events that have been fulfilled among us, just as they were handed on to us by those who from the beginning were eyewitnesses and servants of the word, I too decided, after investigating everything carefully from the very first, to write an orderly account for you, most excellent Theophilus, so that you may know the truth concerning the things about which you have been instructed.*

LUKE 1:1–4

# 3

# Disciples
# and the Sacraments

## Baptism

### General Briefing

Somewhere between two Palestinian seas, Jesus stepped into the waters of the river Jordan and was baptized. Because that event marked the beginning of his ministry, it has frequently been interpreted as his "ordination." With that seemingly simple act, Christ instituted a holy sacrament that, through two thousand years of practice, has grown complex in meaning and diverse in form.

Long religious tradition proclaims that through baptism we are cleansed of sin; relieved of the burden of guilt; and reminded of Christ's death, burial, and resurrection as a blood atonement for the sins of all humanity.

As the centuries pass, refined interpretations appear, shaped by changing cultural conditions and new learnings of each ensuing age, influencing the thought of successive generations of theologians. In recent times, theologians expanded dimensions for the meaning of baptism.

- Baptism is viewed as a transaction between God and the individual. It is a vital moment of consecration and covenant wherein God *imparts* through the Spirit the gifts of grace. We respond with the proclamation of our faith and are baptized into Christ, committing our lives to the way of Christ. In the words of Paul: *"I have been crucified*

31

*with Christ; and it is no longer I who live, but it is Christ who lives in me"* (Gal. 2:19b–20a).

- God, through baptism, enacts a spiritual transformation within us; we are saved from an old way of being and are raised into a new way of being. Baptism is a spiritual liberation; we are no longer estranged from God, no longer living in darkness in the midst of life. The "light of the world" enlightens, and *"whoever follows...will have the light of life"* (John 8:12b).

- God, through baptism, purges all things that have diminished the life of our spirit. The old life is buried; new life is born. Baptism represents a clear break with the past, a transformation of the soul, a receiving of grace. Wholeness is achieved, as we become "at-one-ment" with God.

- God, through baptism, brings us into the full fellowship of the church. It identifies us as members of a congregation and, through receiving our gift of the Holy Spirit, we enter into the ministries of the church.

- God, through baptism, creates a bond linking us to the whole people of God. Through this act, we become "ordained to the priesthood of all believers," a part of a new moral order, kindred spirits with the global company of Christians.

### Disciples' Traditions

Somewhere in the hills of western Pennsylvania, during the summer of 1812, Alexander Campbell, his wife, mother, and father, stepped into the waters of Buffalo Creek and were immersed in baptism. The act resulted from careful study and from Campbell's conclusion that persons baptized in New Testament times were responsible believers and were *immersed.* By consensus rather than formal declaration, those who founded the Disciples' Movement rejected infant baptism and adopted immersion as the accepted form. The question of fellowship with the un-immersed was a source of controversy for a century and more. Ultimately, the moderate views of Barton Stone prevailed, with the acceptance of mutual recognition for *all* who are baptized into Christ and belong to the people of the one God.

Disciples believe that through baptism the church defines itself. The baptismal ceremony marks the line between the church and the world. Baptism is seen as a rite of the church that is *conferred* rather than chosen. The primary act is God's, and we respond through voluntary testimony of faith in Christ. In this act, the ideals and responsibilities of Christian community are infused into the spirit of the new Christian.

Disciples do not impose a "doctrine of baptism" upon members, protecting their freedom to interpret the meaning of baptism for themselves. Generally, Disciples accept immersion as the baptismal form and welcome becoming part of both a congregational community of faith and a global community of faith. Through baptism, Disciples hold that God assures us of the "grace of God," touches us personally with divine love, claims us for a new life, and ordains us to a life in Christ.

### Disciples' Affirmations

Through baptism into Christ we enter into newness of life and are made one with the whole people of God.

THE DESIGN

We, the Christian Church (Disciples of Christ), confess that all who are baptized into Christ are members of His Universal Church and belong to and share in His ministry through the People of the One God.

RESOLUTION 7560–GENERAL ASSEMBLY, 1975

"TOWARD THE MUTUAL RECOGNITION OF MEMBERS"

### Scriptures

*In those days Jesus came from Nazareth of Galilee and was baptized by John in the Jordan. And just as he was coming up out of the water, he saw the heavens torn apart and the Spirit descending like a dove on him. And a voice came from heaven, "You are my Son, the Beloved; with you I am well pleased.*

MARK 1:9–11

*…all of us who have been baptized into Christ Jesus were baptized into his death… [W]e have been buried with him by baptism into death, so that, just as Christ was raised from the dead by the glory of the Father, so we too might walk in newness of life.*

ROMANS 6:3–4

*I have been crucified with Christ; and it is no longer I who live, but… Christ who lives in me. And the life I now live in the flesh, I live by faith in the Son of God.*

GALATIANS 2:19b–20

*"Go therefore and make disciples of all nations, baptizing them in the name of the Father and of the Son and of the Holy Spirit…"*

MATTHEW 28:19

*Peter said to them, "Repent, and be baptized every one of you in the name of Jesus Christ so that your sins may be forgiven; and you will receive the gift of the Holy Spirit."*

ACTS 2:38

*There is one body and one Spirit, just as you were called to the one hope of your calling, one Lord, one faith, one baptism, one God and Father of all, who is above all and through all and in all.*

EPHESIANS 4:4–6

*[B]aptism…saves you—not as a removal of dirt from the body, but as an appeal to God for a good conscience, through the resurrection of Jesus Christ….*

1 PETER 3:21

# The Lord's Supper

## General Briefing

Around 54 C.E., a little community of believers at Corinth was urged by the apostle Paul to rekindle the spirit and essence of the supper instituted by Jesus. Paul's compelling description of the Lord's Supper enshrined it as the most sacred tradition of the church. Known by many names—Holy Communion, Eucharist, Lord's Supper, Lord's Table—it is practiced across Christianity today with varying regularity and form.

Participation in the sacrament of communion, often identified as an ordinance, embraces a broad range of meaning. Christianity has long embraced the tradition regarding the Lord's Supper that God, through our sharing of bread and wine ("my body...my blood"), reminds us of the death and resurrection of Christ, and the sacrifice of Christ's life. The Lord's Supper is viewed as a time of self-examination, personal confession of sin, and receiving God's grace and forgiveness.

Thought and writing of more recent theologians suggest the very life of the church flows through this sacrament—referred to by some as the church's "act of self realization."

- The church gathered at the Lord's Supper is the image and realization of the body of Christ.

- Through the Lord's Supper, God helps us *receive* the living Christ. We affirm the presence of the living Lord and proclaim him the dominant power in our lives.

- The Lord's Supper is an act of thanksgiving for the renewal of our lives in the gift of Christ's Spirit. We pledge faithfulness and reaffirm the covenant of new life conferred upon us by God at baptism.

- The Lord's Supper is a shared meal, revealing openness and acceptance. In the name of an open table, Christianity breaks down the barriers that exclude and separate.

- The Lord's Supper is celebrated in fellowship with the whole people of God. It is an expression of unity, of oneness in Christ, uniting all to one another in the communion of the Holy Spirit. The Lord's Supper is the manifestation of the unity of the people of God gathered by Christ, in Christ.

- The Lord's Supper is a "means of Grace."

## Disciples' Traditions

In the late spring of 1811, a little community of believers at Brush Run, urged by Thomas Campbell, rekindled the spirit and origin of the Lord's Supper. As they sought to restore the essence of the New Testament church, the practice of Holy Communion became the central and distinctive element of worship within Disciples tradition. By mutual agreement rather than denominational edict, the Lord's Supper is offered every Sunday, and on several special gatherings of the congregation such as Christmas Eve and Maundy Thursday. Chosen members of the congregation administer it, most often with an ordained minister presiding. The Lord is the host of the table, open to all who confess that Jesus Christ is Lord. The extraordinary significance of the Lord's Supper to Disciples is apparent in the designation of a chalice as the focal point of the denominational symbol.

As with baptism, Disciples do not impose a doctrine or creed governing the meaning of the Lord's Supper. Each member shares in the communion service guided by his or her own private reflections on its meaning for his or her life.

## Disciples' Affirmations

At the table of the Lord we celebrate with thanksgiving the saving acts and presence of Christ.

THE DESIGN

We are Disciples of Christ, a movement for wholeness in a fragmented world. As part of the one body of Christ, we welcome all to the Lord's Table as God has welcomed us.

DISCIPLES STATEMENT OF IDENTITY

## Scriptures

*While they were eating, he took a loaf of bread, and after blessing it he broke it, gave it to them, and said, "Take; this is my body." Then he took a cup, and after giving thanks he gave it to them, and all of them*

*drank from it. He said to them, "This is my blood of the covenant, which is poured out for many. Truly I will never again drink of the fruit of the vine until that day when I drink it new in the kingdom of God."*
MARK 14:22–25

*For I received from the Lord what I also handed on to you, that the Lord Jesus on the night when he was betrayed took a loaf of bread, and when he had given thanks, he broke it and said, "This is my body that is for you. Do this in remembrance of me." In the same way he took the cup also, after supper, saying, "This cup is the new covenant in my blood. Do this, as often as you drink it, in remembrance of me."*
1 CORINTHIANS 11:23–25

*On the first day of the week, when we met to break bread....*
ACTS 20:7A

*They devoted themselves to the apostles' teaching and fellowship, to the breaking of bread and the prayers... Day by day, as they spent much time together in the temple, they broke bread at home and ate their food with glad and generous hearts. . . .*
ACTS 2:42, 46

# 4

# Disciples at Worship

## Worship

### General Briefing

The scriptures record that Abraham "moved his tent, and came and settled by the oaks of Mamre,...and there he built an altar to the LORD" (Gen. 13:18). That same chapter of scripture records that Lot pitched his tent toward Sodom (13:12). The sharply contrasting decisions of Abraham and Lot reveal an ageless truth: to worship is a free choice.

The choice to worship has been exercised by all cultures in all ages, and the gods have been many. Throughout the epochs of human history, religious bodies have found that careful attention to acts of worship can enrich the lives of a whole people. The individual choice of placing an altar of worship at the center of life is a decisive act that carries far-reaching implications for persons and for entire civilizations.

The character of worship in New Testament times, as determined from limited evidence, was simple and unadorned. Offered in homes and on occasion in catacombs, early Christian worship consisted generally of fellowship, thanksgiving, praying, singing praise to God, proclaiming the gospel, and breaking bread. With the passage of centuries, the style of worship took on the sophistication of ritual, liturgy, costume, and visual images, and was conducted in massive cathedrals by professional clergy. Reaction to this long-practiced style came from theologians who suggested that people at worship should be more than mere spectators viewing a performance, and that clergy and choirs should be thought of as prompters in the wings for the worshipers, who are the actual center-stage participants. The character of worship among religious bodies today offers considerable variety, ranging from settings of elaborate high-church ritual to settings of simple and casual community gatherings, depending largely on local socio-cultural preference.

## Disciples' Traditions

History records that the Campbells and Stone built crude houses to the Lord. Intent upon restoring the simplicity of New Testament worship, the early Disciples and Christians were Spartan in the design and construction of their church buildings and in the structure of their worship services. The appearance of carpets, organs, crosses, and ornamental architectural designs was not common until the Victorian era of the late nineteenth century.

Worship services in early Disciples churches generally included periods for praising God, reading the Bible, praying, taking an offering, sharing in the Lord's Supper, listening to a sermon, and offering an invitation to discipleship. These have remained the basic ingredients of worship for Disciples throughout their history. Alexander Campbell believed that the sequence in which those worship activities occurred was not important, and he therefore urged each congregation to order its worship as it chose. Rather than achieving their goal of restoring New Testament simplicity, it is more accurate to say that Disciples succeeded in adapting a Calvinist or free-church style of worship.

Some authorities suggest that modern Disciples' worship contains two primary elements: the Word and the sacraments, or God speaking and humans responding. Others offer a more complete description of the Disciples' style of worship that includes (1) the *adoration* of God through song, (2) a reverent expression of *thanksgiving* through prayer and gifts, (3) *proclaiming* God through scripture and sermon, (4) receiving God's *renewal* and *benediction* through the sacraments, and (5) participation through joyous *fellowship* with the whole people of God. The evangelistic heritage is reclaimed in the "invitation hymn," which elicits calls to confession of Jesus' lordship and recommitment to one's faith.

More than all else, congregations are communities of worship. They gather on the first day of every week to celebrate the good news and glorify God through adoration and "thankful praise." The moment of worship touches the core of our being where all issues are joined. It is a moment when we search for the deeper meaning of God, set our purpose in perspective, and seek a transformation of the egocentric self that frustrates our best insights and highest resolves. It is a moment that expands our souls.

### Disciples' Affirmations

In the bonds of Christian faith we yield ourselves to God that we may serve the One whose kingdom has no end. Blessing, glory and honor be to God forever.

THE DESIGN

### Scriptures

*"God is spirit, and those who worship him must worship in spirit and truth."*

JOHN 4:24

*They devoted themselves to the apostles' teaching and fellowship, to the breaking of bread and the prayers.*

ACTS 2:42

*[B]e filled with the Spirit, as you sing psalms and hymns and spiritual songs among yourselves, singing and making melody to the Lord in your hearts, giving thanks to God the Father at all times and for everything in the name of our Lord Jesus Christ.*

EPHESIANS 5:18B–20

# Prayer

## General Briefing

The scriptures brim with the language of prayer. The eloquence of prayer is found in the Psalms, in Job, and in the lamentations of the prophets; its perfection, in the prayers of Christ. It is the only language that expresses the full depth and breadth of our lives.

Prayer is the means through which humankind intimately relates to God. Often defined as "communion with God," prayer opens the heart and mind to receive the touch of grace, to liberate the soul from the sag of mediocrity. It is intensely personal, the most critical and essential experience in the life of Christian faith.

Public worship provides sacramental prayer in many forms. There are prayers of *adoration* through which God is praised and glorified. Prayers of *thanksgiving,* often spontaneous, express gratitude for the love of God given in so many ways to all people. There are prayers of *contemplation,* tranquil moments of meditation, frequently in silence, when the soul rests and reflects. Prayers of *confession* provide moments to present ourselves as we are, strength and flaw, wisdom and folly, and to submit to the truth of God. The prayers of *intercession* are given for the sake of others and reflect our appreciation of the dreams and struggles, the joy and sorrow of other people. Prayers of *petition* contain our personal requests for God's blessing, a form of prayer affirmed by Christ's words, "Ask, and it will be given you" (Mt. 7:7). Supremely important are prayers of *submission,* through which we bring our wills into harmony with God's will, especially when we pray, "Your will be done" (Mt. 6:10). Through the richness of these variations of prayer, we are able to know God. It is said prayer is the practice of the presence of God. It is free of magic and miracle–not an attempt to *change* reality, but to *approach* reality differently through loving, caring, sharing: the essence of prayer.

## Disciples' Traditions

Disciples have always viewed prayer as the major discipline of the Christian life. The emphasis has been more upon private prayer than upon a formalized public ordering of prayer in worship. It has been the way through which the personalization of faith has been perceived and practiced over the course of Disciples experience. As a means of enriching the Disciples' personal life in God's presence, there has been much activity: in the publication of devotional literature such as *The Secret Place* and *Fellowship of Prayer,* the distribution of materials to assist in individual Bible study, the encouragement of family devotions, and the emphasis upon preserving private time for reflection.

The private nature of prayer among Disciples has always been supplemented with participation in public worship, keeping the private experience from descending into a sentimental self-centeredness. Listen carefully, and one will note that Disciples prayers in the public sanctuary and in the privacy of the heart are dominated by thankfulness.

## Scriptures

*"Pray then in this way:*
*Our Father in heaven, / hallowed be your name. / Your kingdom come. / Your will be done, / on earth as it is in heaven. / Give us this day our daily bread. / And forgive us our debts, / as we also have forgiven our debtors. / And do not bring us to the time of trial, / but rescue us from the evil one."*

MATTHEW 6:9–13

*"Two men went up to the temple to pray, one a Pharisee and the other a tax collector. The Pharisee, standing by himself, was praying thus, 'God, I thank you that I am not like other people: thieves, rogues, adulterers, or even like this tax collector. I fast twice a week; I give a tenth of all my income.' But the tax collector, standing far off, would not even look up to heaven, but was beating his breast and saying, 'God, be merciful to me, a sinner!' I tell you, this man went down to his home justified*

# 5

# Disciples and Mission

## Search for Unity

### General Briefing

The New Testament church was an informal fellowship of those who believed in Jesus Christ. Communities of Christians took root throughout much of the Mediterranean world. There was not a single "Christianity," but *many* Christianities–no unifying structure, no uniform pattern of local organization, no constituted order of clergy, and no standard theology beyond faith in Jesus Christ. Historical inertia had not yet carried the church through its natural growth toward organization because it had not at that moment recognized either long-range or large-scale tasks. Unity was lodged in spirit and in the lordship of Jesus Christ. Christianity understood itself, however, as being called to *universal* mission and to be intrinsically ecumenical in its character.

As the centuries passed, the church became increasingly institutionalized around a system of beliefs determined and defended by a clerical class. During the sixteenth-century Protestant Reformation, the formalized church of Western Europe was displaced by a pattern of diverse national religions continuing the medieval alliance of church and state. Following the Protestant Reformation, Christianity suffered repeated fragmentation born of differing understandings of faith and traditions. A few scattered, courageous voices attempted to give ecumenical witness during the decades that followed, but issues of doctrine and polity always overpowered the advocacy for Christian unity; and the revolutionary political reforms of later centuries spawned a new denominational system, a system less conducive to Christian unity.

## Disciples' Traditions

The ardent impulse for Christian unity has been in the bloodline of the Christian Church (Disciples of Christ) through two centuries of its lineage. The concept of unity has taken new form with each generation, evolving out of the early nineteenth-century mix of religious fragments in local communities, to a twentieth-century design of universal corporate structures, to the present quest for union embracing diversity—"a legitimate diversity of our given oneness."

With the hope of achieving peace and harmony in the communities they served, Barton Stone and Thomas Campbell sought an underlying unity of spirit and character among the disparate pieces of the church. Stone thought of himself and his followers as peacemakers, reducing denominational divisions and following the *polar star* of unity onto the common ground of Christ. Thomas Campbell condemned the "heinous nature… of religious controversy among Christians," but recognized that the church must exist in locally separate and distinct societies. In one of the most important statements in the whole history of ecumenism, Campbell offered his belief that "uncharitable division" was avoidable by accepting the principle that *the church of Christ upon earth is essentially, intentionally, and constitutionally one.* The intense passion for unity often came into conflict with the more intense passion for individual expressions of faith, a conflict that has repeatedly blunted unity initiatives. The Stone and Campbell Movements eventually joined in a union made possible by its localism and the elastic quality of its organization that allowed for diversity. It was the first and last instance of full union to occur in Disciples history within the United States and Canada.

The *polar star* of unity became clouded for a time during the late 1800s as the Stone-Campbell Movement concentrated its energies upon the restoration of the New Testament church. The restoration effort led to divisiveness rather than unity, producing three distinct denominations.

Under the prophetic guidance of such leaders as Peter Ainslie, Charles Clayton Morrison, George G. Beazley Jr., Paul A. Crow Jr., Robert Welsh, and Michael Kinnamon, the Christian Church (Disciples of Christ) has become recognized as one of the most forceful voices in Christianity promoting ecumenical reform throughout the twentieth and into the twentieth-first centuries. Disciples have actively related to all major conciliar structures, including the Federal Council of Churches (1908), the World Council of Churches (1948), and the National Council of Churches (1950). In 1910, the Disciples formed the Council on Christian Union, now the Council on Christian Unity, which was the first ecumenical agency of its kind created by a denomination to cultivate the ideal of unity.

Disciples have followed the *polar star* into numerous conversations toward corporate union on a grand scale. These efforts have included the Philadelphia Plan (1918), the Greenwich Plan (1946–1957), conversations with American Baptists (1940s–1950s), and conversations with the United Church of Christ leading to a Declaration of Full Communion (1961–1966, 1977, 1985, and 1989). In other comprehensive efforts, Disciples were one of the founders of The World Convention of Christian Churches in 1930, and the Consultation on Church Union in 1962–which, in 2002, became the Churches Uniting in Christ. Disciples were also among the founders in 2001 of the Christian Churches Together in the USA, and joined in conversations among the three branches of the Stone-Campbell Dialogue.

As we live into the twenty-first century, the *polar star* of the Christian Church (Disciples of Christ) remains undimmed. The quest for unity proceeds as a quest refined through a new identity statement: "*We are Disciples of Christ, a movement for wholeness in a fragmented world. As part of the one body of Christ, we welcome all to the Lord's Table as God as welcomed us."* It is a quest for a unity through common faith in Christ, a unity of humankind, a unity in freedom, a unity that comprehends a vast diversity, a unity linked to prophetic witness and service.

## Disciples' Affirmations

We will, that this body die, be dissolved, and sink into union with the Body of Christ at large; for there is but one Body, and one Spirit, even as we are called in one hope of our calling,

*The Last Will and Testament of the Springfield Presbytery (1804)*

That the church of Christ upon earth is essentially, intentionally, and constitutionally one; consisting of all those in every place that profess their faith in Christ.

DECLARATION AND ADDRESS (1809)

Within the whole family of God on earth, the church appears wherever believers in Jesus Christ are gathered in His name.

THE DESIGN

## Scriptures

*"I ask not only on behalf of these, but also on behalf of those who will believe in me through their word, that they may all be one.*

JOHN 17:20–21A

*There is one body and one Spirit, just as you were called to the one hope of your calling, one Lord, one faith, one baptism, one God and Father of all, who is above all and through all and in all.*

EPHESIANS 4:4–6

*Now I appeal to you, brothers and sisters, by the name of our Lord Jesus Christ, that all of you be in agreement and that there be no divisions among you, but that you be united in the same mind and the same purpose. For it has been reported to me by Chloe's people that there are quarrels among you, my brothers and sisters. What I mean is that each of you says, "I belong to Paul," or "I belong to Apollos," or "I belong to Cephas," or "I belong to Christ." Has Christ been divided?*

1 CORINTHIANS 1:10–13A

# Global Mission

## General Briefing

Some of the last words of Jesus Christ to his disciples were, "Go therefore and make disciples of all nations…".(Mt. 28:19). Responding to this great commission, the apostles traveled their separate directions across the known world, proclaiming Christ. Their message transcended nation, race, class, and culture. All persons on earth were seen as children of God and bound together as the whole people of God through faith in Jesus Christ.

## Disciples' Traditions

The Stone-Campbell Movement was among the leaders of Protestantism in developing a network of overseas missions. As early as 1849 the Movement had dispatched missionaries to Jerusalem. By 1918 the number of missionaries totaled 185 persons, stationed in all corners of the earth. Key leaders of that mission thrust were Caroline Neville Pearre of the Christian Woman's Board of Missions and Archibald McLean of the Foreign Christian Missionary Society.

The character of Disciples mission work during the nineteenth and early twentieth centuries was largely evangelistic and denominational. Congregations and individuals generously supported the effort by contributing funds, accepting living-link missionaries, and donating the endowment to found a College of Missions for the training of missionaries. Although the formation of the United Christian Missionary Society in 1919 combined home and overseas programs as a single mission, the character and thrust of the foreign mission segment remained substantially unchanged through World War II.

A watershed in the Disciples mission effort was reached in 1959 with the approval of a policy statement designed by A. Dale Fiers and Virgil Sly, titled "Strategy of World Mission: Basic Policy of the Division of World Mission of the United Christian Missionary Society." This new statement was born of the reaction against the smothering effects of denominationalism, colonialism, and imperialism upon church mission. Couched in an affirmation of human dignity, freedom, and economic justice as legitimate concerns of the Christian faith, the statement declared that the mission effort should intimately relate to the life of the people by assisting in the development of indigenous forms of worship, leadership, organization, and theology. It was bold in its call to abandon the "old possessiveness" and to pursue mission in an ecumenical context with a multiform purpose of proclamation, fellowship, and service. It was the express intent of this innovative strategy to be mobile, flexible, and open-ended. Through the work of Robert A. Thomas, Disciples ratified this shift of mission focus in their 1981 General Assembly.

Implementation of the new strategy transformed the character of the Disciples foreign mission program. New overseas personnel are sent not on initiative from the Christian Church (Disciples of Christ), but in response to requests from the churches in the lands where they would serve. They are selected on the basis of a specific expertise required in a particular setting and situation, placed on short-term assignment, and often financed by ecumenical pools. As of 2016, the overseas staff of the Christian Church (Disciples of Christ), working jointly with the United Church of Christ, consisted of 110 personnel in 42 countries: 33 fully-supported missionaries, 23 long-term volunteers, 14 global mission interns, and 40 overseas associates (UCC and Disciples working with global partners under their auspices). Of the 60 administrative staff, 19 were educators, 9 were in health care, 12 worked in community development, and the remainder served in a variety of positions to support and strengthen our partner churches and church-related organizations.

In 1996 the Division of Overseas Ministries and the Wider Church Ministries of the United Church of Christ formed the Common Global Ministries Board of the Christian Church

(Disciples of Christ) and the United Church of Christ, thereby creating a common policy-making body for both denominations and joining the staffs of both churches as an expression of partnership. And the National Council of the Churches of Christ in the United States of America provides numerous channels through which the Christian Church (Disciples of Christ) participates in common global ministries.

The restructure process of the late 1960s altered the organizational character of Disciples' administration of overseas ministries. The United Christian Missionary Society was converted to a holding company and two new divisions, integrally related to the church, were created: the Division of Overseas Ministries and the Division of Homeland Ministries (now Disciples Home Missions). Through the Division of Overseas Ministries, the Christian Church (Disciples of Christ) deals directly with sister churches overseas. This church-to-church directness, as contrasted with missionary societies to church, represents a dramatic change of relationship, a concept pioneered by Disciples. The new concept has enabled the Christian Church (Disciples of Christ) "to participate faithfully in Christ's ministry of witness, service and reconciliation in the whole world," and to renew its effort to fulfill Christ's ancient commission.

## Disciples' Affirmations

As Disciples, we believe God calls us to be and to share the Good News of Jesus Christ, witnessing, loving and serving from our doorsteps "to the ends of the earth".

THE DESIGN

UPDATED JULY 2005

## Scriptures

*"All authority in heaven and on earth has been given to me. Go therefore and make disciples of all nations, baptizing them in the name of the Father and of the Son and of the Holy Spirit, and teaching them to*

*obey everything that I have commanded you. And remember, I am with you always, to the end of the age."*

MATTHEW 28:18B–20

*"...and you will be my witnesses in Jerusalem, in all Judea and Samaria, and to the ends of the earth."*

ACTS 1:8B

# 6

# Disciples and Moral-Ethical Issues

## Disciples' Traditions

From their origins as a rural people and their belief in the sovereignty of individual choice, Disciples were slow to develop a collective social justice consciousness. Socially isolated and concentrating upon missionary efforts along with their own growth as a movement, they assigned lower priority to the moral-ethical questions in the society around them. Lacking a unified voice or representative structure and fearing division within the growing Movement, Disciples did not speak forcefully on issues such as Indian Removal or Slavery. Scholars believe that early generations of Disciples were poorly prepared theologically to confront the religious and moral implications of racism and war.

The rapid industrialization of America during the final decades of the nineteenth century spawned a wide range of social issues that awakened a new moral concern among Disciples. Among those issues were violent disputes between labor and management, the quality of life in a rapidly urbanizing society, growing classes of economically and politically oppressed persons, and a broad array of questions in the area of human and civil rights. Sensitized by these social disorders, Disciples debated whether the role of the church was to evangelize persons or to engage actively in efforts to change the social environment. In general, Disciples' concern for unity continued to overpower their concern for social justice.

Although nineteenth-century Disciples rarely spoke with one voice on controversial social questions, there was one striking exception. A major issue of that era was the manufacture and sale of liquor, which Disciples universally opposed and against which they exerted political influence wherever possible. The sensational exploits of Carry Nation brought national attention to the Disciples and to their staunch support of prohibition.

Following the 1968 adoption of the covenantal *Design,* the Christian Church (Disciples of Christ), for the first time, had a representative means for speaking as a church and proceeded to do so regularly. In its twenty-four General Assemblies (1969–2015) since that time, the church has spoken 338 times through formal resolutions on moral-ethical issues of the day. This accounts for nearly one-third of all official actions of the church during the near fifty-year period, a fact that attests to a social awareness and to a willingness on the part of Disciples to use their collective voice to influence the social environment. However, these declarations never presume to speak for *all* Disciples, a frequently misunderstood fact. Resolutions on moral-ethical issues call the church to study and to engagement, but do not impose universally held positions on its members.

That is one aspect of Disciples' tenacity in defending the freedom of individual opinion. Hearkening back to the impetus for their own founding, Disciples are still a people quick to challenge any source of authority that does not begin with an act of individual choice. An example of this continuing Disciples tradition is illustrated in the 1975 resolution concerning the still-controversial issue of abortion. The resolution was labeled "Concerning Individual Freedom in Abortion Decisions" and contained the following resolves:

1.  *Affirm* the principle of individual liberty, freedom of individual conscience, and sacredness of life for all persons.

2. *Respect differences* in religious beliefs concerning abortion and oppose, in accord with the principle of religious liberty, in any attempt to legislate a specific religious opinion or belief concerning abortion upon all Americans.

While Disciples as a body may disapprove of the general practice of abortion, they recognize a greater danger of legislating a single moral opinion for all persons, thereby abridging the freedom of individual choice. On moral-ethical questions related to personal behavior, Disciples tend to affirm and reaffirm this position, which is a cherished part of their heritage.

On the other hand, the General Assembly of the Christian Church (Disciples of Christ) frequently takes a definitive stand on matters affecting the government of the social community at large. On the question of capital punishment, the Disciples passed resolutions in 1957, 1962, 1973, 1975, and 1991 through which the church repeatedly reaffirmed "its historic stand against capital punishment and calls upon its members to oppose attempts to legislate it."

The church, through its General Assembly, addressed a broad range of social justice issues during the nearly five decades from 1969 to 2015.

| SUBJECT | NUMBER OF RESOLUTIONS | | | | |
|---|---|---|---|---|---|
| | 1969-79 | 1981-89 | 1991-2001 | 2003-15 | Totals |
| Disciples Priorities | 3 | 3 | 1 | 1 | 8 |
| Biomedical Ethics | 0 | 4 | 1 | 0 | 5 |
| Civil Liberties | 4 | 0 | 1 | 5 | 15 |
| Criminal Justice | 4 | 1 | 2 | 2 | 9 |
| Ecology & Lifestyle | 5 | 11 | 4 | 1 | 20 |
| Family | 9 | 7 | 3 | 0 | 19 |
| Gun Control | 2 | 1 | 0 | 1 | 4 |
| Health Care | 3 | 1 | 5 | 7 | 16 |
| Human Rights | 6 | 2 | 4 | 1 | 13 |

| | | | | | |
|---|---|---|---|---|---|
| Human Hunger | 8 | 2 | 0 | 0 | 10 |
| Immigration, Refugees | 1 | 7 | 0 | 5 | 13 |
| International Relations | 13 | 27 | 20 | 6 | 66 |
| Labor Relations | 6 | 2 | 1 | 2 | 11 |
| Language | 0 | 1 | 1 | 1 | 3 |
| Mass Media, TV | 2 | 0 | 0 | 0 | 2 |
| Morality, Public & Private | 9 | 6 | 0 | 0 | 15 |
| Peace & War | 13 | 19 | 6 | 12 | 50 |
| Racial/Ethnic Issues | 2 | 7 | 6 | 5 | 20 |
| Sexuality | 1 | 14 | 6 | 4 | 25 |
| United Nations | 2 | 0 | 2 | 0 | 4 |
| Urbanization | 1 | 0 | 2 | 0 | 3 |
| Voluntary Services | 0 | 2 | 1 | 0 | 3 |
| Poverty, Welfare Reform | 4 | 0 | 2 | 0 | 6 |
| Totals | 98 (29%) | 117 (35%) | 68 (20%) | 55 (16%) | 338 (100%) |
| No. of Assemblies | 6 | 5 | 6 | 4 | 24 |
| Ave. # Res. Per Assembly | 16 | 23 | 11 | 7.8 | 14 |

Debate and voting on the 338 resolutions noted above often led to divisiveness within the church. To counter the contention, Disciples in 1993 developed a "process of discernment" to address those particularly controversial issues clearly devoid of consensus. The ideal of discernment was to move the church toward serious study, reflection, and active conversation. In this way, the process could become a resource for every expression of the church to help guide Disciples toward a common course of action in their pursuit of faithfulness. Some who want Disciples to be more proactive on issues of social justice have viewed the process of discernment as a means to avoid taking a stand, a process that weakened the prophetic voice of the church and exhibited less regard for the social justice imperatives of Christianity. Others claim congregations and regions rarely use the discernment process because they wish to avoid controversy. Since the early 1990s, the number of social justice resolutions significantly decreased due in large part to the 1992 dismantling of the six-member *Department of Church in Society* within the former Division of Homeland Ministries–the department that had produced several of the social witness resolutions considered by the various General Assemblies.

As Disciples decreased their use of General Assembly resolutions to address issues of social justice, they increased their use of other ministries within the church such as Disciples Peace Fellowship, Week of Compassion, Refugee and Immigration Ministries, GLAD Alliance, and Reconciliation Ministry–along with the creation of the "Justice Table," which addresses four significant concerns: Women & Children, Immigration, Hunger & Poverty, and Care for the Earth. A passion for social justice continues to find creative expression through the ministries of the Disciples faith community–congregation, region, and general.

Disciples have clearly developed a more vigorous social justice awareness since restructure and are prone to speak forthrightly on issues in the socioeconomic, political, and international arenas. On matters of personal morality, Disciples hold a deep confidence in the ability of individuals to form judgments for themselves. If you ask about the moral correctness of having an abortion, the appropriate expression of human sexuality, seeking a divorce, consuming drugs or alcohol, or participating in any number of other activities that raise questions of an ethical or moral nature, the Christian Church (Disciples of Christ) will not provide a systematic blueprint for your personal behavior. It will, however, insist that you carefully study the moral and ethical teachings of Christ and assume full moral responsibility for your personal decisions.

## Disciples' Affirmations

WHEREAS, many individuals, as well as the culture as a whole, are experiencing confusion concerning the goals of life and principles to guide behavior, as well as the breaking down of patterns, structures, and disciplines that have previously guided them in all aspects of life:

THEREFORE, BE IT RESOLVED, that the (Assembly) declare anew its allegiance to Jesus' summary of the law, that we love God with all our heart, soul, mind, and strength; and that we love our neighbor as ourselves; and

BE IT FURTHER RESOLVED, that the Assembly call upon the members of the Christian Church (Disciples of Christ) to reaffirm this allegiance to the divine will in their prayers, their thinking about morality and ethics, their personal behavior, their public actions, and the activities and teachings of their congregations.

*Concerning Christian Morality (1979)*
*General Assembly Resolution 7956*

## Scriptures

*I therefore, the prisoner in the Lord, beg you to lead a life worthy of the calling to which you have been called...*

EPHESIANS 4:1

*He (Jesus) unrolled the scroll and found the place where it was written: "The Spirit of the Lord is upon me, / because he has anointed me / to bring good news to the poor. / He has sent me to proclaim release to the captives / and recovery of sight to the blind, / to let the oppressed go free, / to proclaim the year of the Lord's favor."*

LUKE 4:17B–19

*Finally, beloved, whatever is true, whatever is honorable, whatever is just, whatever is pure, whatever is pleasing, whatever is commendable, if there is any excellence and if there is anything worthy of praise, think about these things.*

PHILIPPIANS 4:8

*He has told you, O mortal, what is good;*
 *and what does the LORD require of you*
*but to do justice, and to love kindness,*
 *and to walk humbly with your God?*

MICAH 6:8

*What good is it, my brothers and sisters, if you say you have faith but do not have works? Can faith save you? If a brother or sister is naked*

*and lacks daily food, and one of you says to them, "Go in peace; keep warm and eat your fill," and yet you do not supply their bodily needs, what is the good of that? So faith by itself, if it has no works, is dead.*
JAMES 2:14–17

*"Come, you that are blessed by my Father, inherit the kingdom prepared for you from the foundation of the world; for I was hungry and you gave me food, I was thirsty and you gave me something to drink, I was a stranger and you welcomed me, I was naked and you gave me clothing, I was sick and you took care of me, I was in prison and you visited me."*
MATTHEW 25:34–36

# 7

# Disciples and
# Church Structure

## The Ministry

### General Briefing

Pastoral letters of New Testament days circulated among the newly developing communities of believers urging the appointment of leaders for a "noble task." Those appointed were ordinary folk chosen from among the rank-and-file first-century Christians, and they were given various titles, including "elder," "deacon," and "bishop." Such appointments reveal an assertion of trust in the common mind, a view reinforced by the emphasis placed upon character rather than function in the phrases of the pastoral letters.

Over the course of a century, the evolving church gradually replaced its informal ministry with a formalized order of clergy. By Medieval times the function of professional clergy had been systematized into iron uniformity, but soon yielded to a new and broad diversification due to the explosion of church forms sparked by the Protestant Reformation. Across Christianity today, there is the barest of consensus on the way to prioritize four broad categories of ministerial responsibilities:

a. Preaching and teaching

b. Leading worship and administering sacraments

c. Pastoral care to individuals

d. Administering the work of the church

From denomination to denomination, and from congregation to congregation, there is little agreement on the priority of one general category of responsibilities over another. The choice is largely dependent upon the momentary need of each local congregation.

## Disciples' Traditions

Founders of the Disciples Movement developed their notions of ministry out of their disdain for a dominating clergy, their distrust of authority, and their firm belief in the concept of congregational freedom. From the Spirit received through Christ, each congregation was empowered to ordain and employ persons for pastoral leadership. Those chosen for leadership were ordinary folk, summoned from the plough, the village, the shop, the mill, and the kitchen–(Leah Fiers, a pioneer female minister, was ordained in 1895 at Iroquois, Illinois, and later became the mother of A. Dale Fiers.) Nineteenth-century Disciples ministers were enjoined by compact with the local congregation and variously referred to as "messengers," "elders," "deacons," or "evangelists." Disciples tried to walk the line between clerical order and clerical anarchy by declaring the distinction between clergy and laity to be a matter of degree, not kind.

With passing decades, the need for responsible clergy prompted the gradual development of a professional Disciples' ministry that had satisfied the requirements of a specialized theological education and a specific set of qualifications for ordination. Through the process of restructure, a set of guidelines entitled *Policies and Criteria for the Order of Ministry* was developed in 1971 for the church as a whole. Regions authorize ordination and certify the standing of ministers, while congregations retain the right to call their ministers and assume the responsibility to sustain them in faithfulness and honor. The covenant between pastor and congregation is still the conclusive and confirming compact for ministry. A process to revise the *Policies and Criteria* was adopted by the 2009 General Assembly, and set forth in a document titled *Theological Foundations and Policies and Criteria for Ordering of Ministry of the Christian Church (Disciples of Christ)*. Revisions were approved and subsequently implemented on August 1, 2011.

## Disciples' Affirmations

The fundamental ministry within the church is that of Jesus Christ… By virtue of baptism in the church, every Christian enters into the corporate ministry of God's people… In addition, the church recognizes an order of the ministry, set apart under God, to equip the whole people to fulfill their corporate ministry.

THE DESIGN

UPDATED JULY 2005

*The Order of Ministry in the Christian Church (Disciples of Christ) comprises Commissioned Ministers and Ordained Ministers. By Ordination the church recognizes the work of the Holy Spirit in calling particular persons to creative and imaginative servanthood in Christ; accepts their ministry in and for the Christian Church (Disciples of Christ) and for the whole body of Christ; covenants to undergird the ministry; and grants authority to perform that ministry as a representative of the church. Ordained ministers are baptized members of a Disciples congregation.*

***Ordination*** *is a process of the Congregational and Regional Church on behalf of the whole church to commend to Christians everywhere individuals who meet the qualifications and have fulfilled the requirements established by the Christian Church (Disciples of Christ) for Ordination.*

*The candidate shall be recommended for Ordination by a recognized congregation or congregations of the Christian Church (Disciples of Christ), including the one in which membership is held. The service ordinarily shall be held in a sponsoring congregation.*

***Commissioned*** *ministry provides the Church opportunity for creativity and imagination in acknowledging the fresh work of the Holy Spirit. These ministries may include: pastors, evangelists, Christian educators, ministers of music, youth ministers, parish nurses,* *chaplains, bi-vocational ministers...or others where Regional nurture and authorization are deemed appropriate.*

*By virtue of Commissioning or Ordination according to the Order of Ministry of the Christian Church (Disciples of Christ), the minister becomes eligible for Standing.*

*Policies and Criteria for the Ordering of Ministry,* **basic policy** *1971, amended 1977, 1981, 1985, 1987, 1995, and 2009. Selected quotations above are from the Policies and Criteria as amended in 2009.*

## Scriptures

*The gifts he gave were that some would be apostles, some prophets, some evangelists, some pastors and teachers, to equip the saints for the work of ministry, for building up the body of Christ...*

EPHESIANS 4:11–12

*But how are they to call on one in whom they have not believed? And how are they to believe in one of whom they have never heard? And how are they to hear without someone to proclaim him? And how are they to proclaim him unless they are sent? As it is written, "How beautiful are the feet of those who bring good news!"*

ROMANS 10:14–15

*After they had appointed elders for them in each church, with prayer and fasting they entrusted them to the Lord in whom they had come to believe.*

ACTS 14:23

*[W]hoever aspires to the office of bishop desires a noble task. Now a bishop must be above reproach, married only once, temperate, sensible, respectable, hospitable, an apt teacher, not a drunkard, not violent but gentle, not quarrelsome, and not a lover of money. He must manage his own household well, keeping his children submissive and respectful in every way—for if someone does not know how to manage his own household, how can he take care of God's church? He must not be a recent convert, or he may be puffed up with conceit and fall into the condemnation of the devil. Moreover, he must be well thought of by outsiders, so that he may not fall into disgrace and the snare of the devil.*

1 TIMOTHY 3:1–7

*Let the elders who rule well be considered worthy of double honor, especially those who labor in preaching and teaching...*

1 TIMOTHY 5:17

# The Laity

## General Briefing

An emerging laity marched with the religious awakenings through Protestantism during the late eighteenth and most of the nineteenth centuries. Due to the separation of church and state, which placed dependence upon church membership for financial support, laypersons exerted new initiative and were accorded increasingly significant roles in the life of the church. The laity became particularly active in the Sunday school movement, the development of Bible societies, and the creation of Christian associations. So strong did laity become that some theologians referred to the development as the age of "lay Christianity." The principle of the "priesthood of all believers" suddenly moved from abstract theological discussion to a practical reality.

## Disciples' Traditions

The Stone and Campbell Movements were born at the zenith of the awakenings, with their accompanying emancipations of laity. Campbell's Disciples and Stone's Christians alike enshrined the principle of lay sovereignty in their congregations. Recognizing a less than slight distinction between laity and clergy, the early reformers empowered members of the congregations to administer the Lord's Supper, to teach, to preach, and to hold the primary office of elder in their congregational structure.

As national structures evolved from the need to help congregations cooperate with each other in broader purpose, Disciples' laymen and laywomen were frequently chosen to lead and to administer. Laity has maintained its fixed, stable, and formidable position among Disciples into the twenty-first century. Local governing boards and the eldership of each congregation continue to be composed of and led by laity. The highest elective office in the Christian Church (Disciples of Christ) is the moderator, an office filled as often by laypeople as ministers, evidence that the "priesthood of all believers" is a serious matter with Disciples.

Who, and how many, compose the Disciples' laity? While the people as a whole who compose the Christian Church (Disciples of Christ) are older and less cosmopolitan than the nation at large, they represent, in general, a reasonable cross-section of the middle class. The 2000 statistics of the Church as compiled by the Office of Research, compared with the 2000 census report of the United States, offered a context revealing the story of numbers. (An estimated number of young un-baptized children of Disciples parents is included, to help the comparison.)

| AGE GROUP | DISCIPLES | U.S. POPULATION |
|---|---|---|
| 0-4 | 5.0% | 7.2% |
| 5-14 | 12.0% | 14.8% |
| 15-24 | 11.3% | 14.0% |
| 25-34 | 10.1% | 13.5% |
| 35-44 | 15.3% | 16.4% |
| 45-54 | 9.3% | 13.4% |
| 55-64 | 14.0% | 8.5% |
| 65-74 | 13.2% | 6.5% |
| 75-84 | 7.5% | 4.3% |
| 85+ | 2.3% | 1.1% |
| Male | 46.15% | 48.87% |
| Female | 53.85% | 51.13% |

The church is "divine in intention and human in organization," and each generation of the church becomes a contemporary incarnation. First, last, and always, Disciples affirm that the church is people.

## Disciples' Affirmations

Within the whole family of God on earth, the church appears wherever believers in Jesus Christ are gathered in his name.

THE DESIGN

## Scriptures

*For just as the body is one and has many members, and all the members of the body, though many, are one body, so it is with Christ. For in the one Spirit we were all baptized into one body... Now you are the body of Christ and individually members of it.*

1 CORINTHIANS 12:12–13A, 27

# The Design

### Disciples' Traditions

The Stone-Campbell Movement was rooted in an aversion to ecclesiastical authority. Early attempts at cooperation among congregations were associational in character, which limited their effectiveness in creating programs of scale and range. In the free-church tradition, Disciples addressed the questions of organization in pragmatic rather than theological terms. The first twentieth-century effort to improve the organizational efficiency of Disciples was the formation of the International Convention in 1917, an association that was complemented in its work by the United Christian Missionary Society, a consolidation of six independent church agencies.

Disciples made their most telling structural advance with the imaginative development of a covenantal *Design* rather than a formal constitution. Seeking a fuller meaning of church, the theologically based *Design* provided a way for three expressions—congregations, regions, and general ministries—to be voluntarily joined in a covenant binding them to each other and to God. The relationship of the three expressions is one of mutual interdependence, mutual sustenance, and mutual responsibility, with the integrity of each expression carefully protected. There is no pyramid of authority, no top or bottom. It is a design for *one* church, not three, a church flexible, dynamic, and open—developing from within, not overweighted with bureaucratic structures. The basic *Design* was adopted in 1968 as a *Provisional Design;* it was successfully amended in 1969, 1971, 1973, 1975, 1977 (when the word *Provisional* was dropped), 1983, 1985, 1995, and, with significant revisions, in 2005.

## *The Congregational Expression*

Through covenant, the Christian Church (Disciples of Christ) "manifests itself in congregations." Local congregations are organized to help each member participate in the life of the total church and to help the total church function as a whole. Within the corporate structure of the Christian Church (Disciples of Christ), each congregation enjoys specific rights and shares in specific responsibilities. Among the rights safeguarded for each congregation in *The Design* are the right to manage its own affairs, the right to own and control its own property, the right to constitute its own corporate organizational structure and name, the right to call its own minister, the right to set its own financial policies, and the right to participate through its chosen representatives in forming the corporate judgments of the total church. Freedom is always accompanied by responsibility. Among the responsibilities cited in *The Design* for each congregation are the responsibility to administer baptism and the Lord's Supper, the responsibility to sustain its minister faithfully and with honor, the responsibility for effective stewardship in the work of the total church, and the responsibility to view the church as a universal fellowship.

## *The Regional Expression*

By virtue of membership in a recognized local congregation, a Disciple also holds membership in the region where the congregation is located. There are thirty-two geographical units, called regions, within the Christian Church (Disciples of Christ), each charged with functions under the broad categories of mission and nurture. The region of Canada, with 25 congregations and 1,500 members, contains a dual character— as both a region and a nation. The use of the word "general" rather than "national" when referring to ministries within *The Christian Church (Disciples of Christ ) in the United States and*

*Canada* honors this cooperative relationship. Regional *mission* responsibility includes leading in the development of a sensitive comprehension of human needs beyond the congregation, leading in the discovery of new forms of ministerial witness, and leading in the pursuit of ecumenical means to fulfill mission. Regional *nurture* responsibilities are more specific, and include certifying the standing of ministers, providing pastoral care for ministers and congregations, overseeing the process of ordination and relocation of ministers, and assisting each congregation to relate to the general expression of church. Each region, like each congregation, reserves certain rights to itself, such as constituting its own board, by-laws, and budget; owning its own property; calling its ministerial staff; and being represented in the process of developing the corporate judgments of the total church. An accompanying map illustrates the geographic configuration of the regional expression of the Christian Church (Disciples of Christ).

### The General Expression

Each member of a local Disciples congregation is thereby a member of the Christian Church (Disciples of Christ) as a whole, which expresses itself in the United States and Canada through a general organization called the General Assembly. This is a representative biennial gathering that reflects the wholeness and unity of the total church. Through this assembly, the Christian Church (Disciples of Christ) is enabled to speak to the world with one voice on socioeconomic concerns and human needs, to oversee the work of the church's respective ministries, and to lay the basis for cooperating with other religious bodies in fulfilling a common mission of witness and service.

To inform and implement its work, the General Assembly looks to its three non-salaried officers, identified as moderators; a salaried chief executive officer, designated as the general minister and president for the whole church; a general board consisting of 125 members (62 voting); and eleven administrative units, each responsible for specified administrative functions, study, and service. While these components are under the general supervision of the assembly, they also function for the whole of the covenanted expressions (congregations, regions, general) as well as to other religious bodies and to ecumenical structures. For a graphic explanation of this unique *Design,* you will be assisted by the structure chart that follows.

## Disciples' Affirmations

As a member of the whole body of Christ, every person who is or shall become a member of a recognized congregation of the Christian Church (Disciples of Christ) thereby holds membership in the region in which that congregation is located and in the Christian Church (Disciples of Christ) in the United States and Canada.

The nature of the church, given by Christ, remains constant through the generations; yet in faithfulness to its mission, it continues to adapt its structures to the needs and patterns of a changing world. All dominion in the church belongs to Jesus Christ, its Lord and Head, and any exercise of authority in the church on earth stands under His judgment.

THE DESIGN

## Scriptures

*But speaking the truth in love, we must grow up in every way into him who is the head, into Christ, from whom the whole body, joined and knit together by every ligament with which it is equipped, as each part is working properly, promotes the body's growth in building itself up in love.*

EPHESIANS 4:15–16

*For as in one body we have many members, and not all the members have the same function, so we, who are many, are one body in Christ, and individually we are members one of another.*

ROMANS 12:4–5

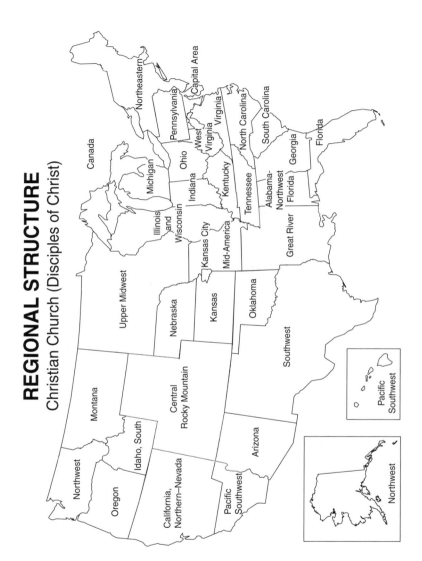

**REGIONAL STRUCTURE**
Christian Church (Disciples of Christ)

This map has been provided courtesy of the Office of the General Minister and President of the Christian Church (Disciples of Christ), Indianapolis, Indiana.

# General Ministries and Racial/Ethnic Ministries

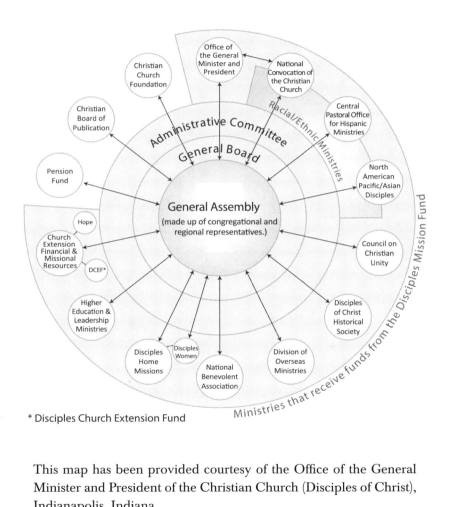

* Disciples Church Extension Fund

This map has been provided courtesy of the Office of the General Minister and President of the Christian Church (Disciples of Christ), Indianapolis, Indiana.